DECODABLE BOOK 23

SCHOOL PUBLISHERS

Copyright © by Harcourt, Inc.

All rights reserved. No part of this publication may be reproduced or transmitted in any form or by any means, electronic or mechanical, including photocopy, recording, or any information storage and retrieval system, without permission in writing from the publisher.

Requests for permission to make copies of any part of the work should be addressed to School Permissions and Copyrights, Harcourt, Inc., 6277 Sea Harbor Drive, Orlando, Florida 32887-6777. Fax: 407-345-2418.

HARCOURT and the Harcourt Logo are trademarks of Harcourt, Inc., registered in the United States of America and/or other jurisdictions.

Printed in China

ISBN 10 0-15-364139-8

ISBN 13 978-0-15-364139-8

6 7 8 9 10   0940   17 16 15 14 13 12 11 10 09

Ordering Options
ISBN 10 0-15-364241-6
ISBN 13 978-0-15-364241-8

If you have received these materials as examination copies free of charge, Harcourt School Publishers retains title to the materials and they may not be resold. Resale of examination copies is strictly prohibited and is illegal.

Possession of this publication in print format does not entitle users to convert this publication, or any portion of it, into electronic format.

Contents

Waldo Wins 1
   Vowel Variant /ô/ *a(l), ough*

At the Ballpark 9
   Vowel Variant /ô/ *a(l), ough*

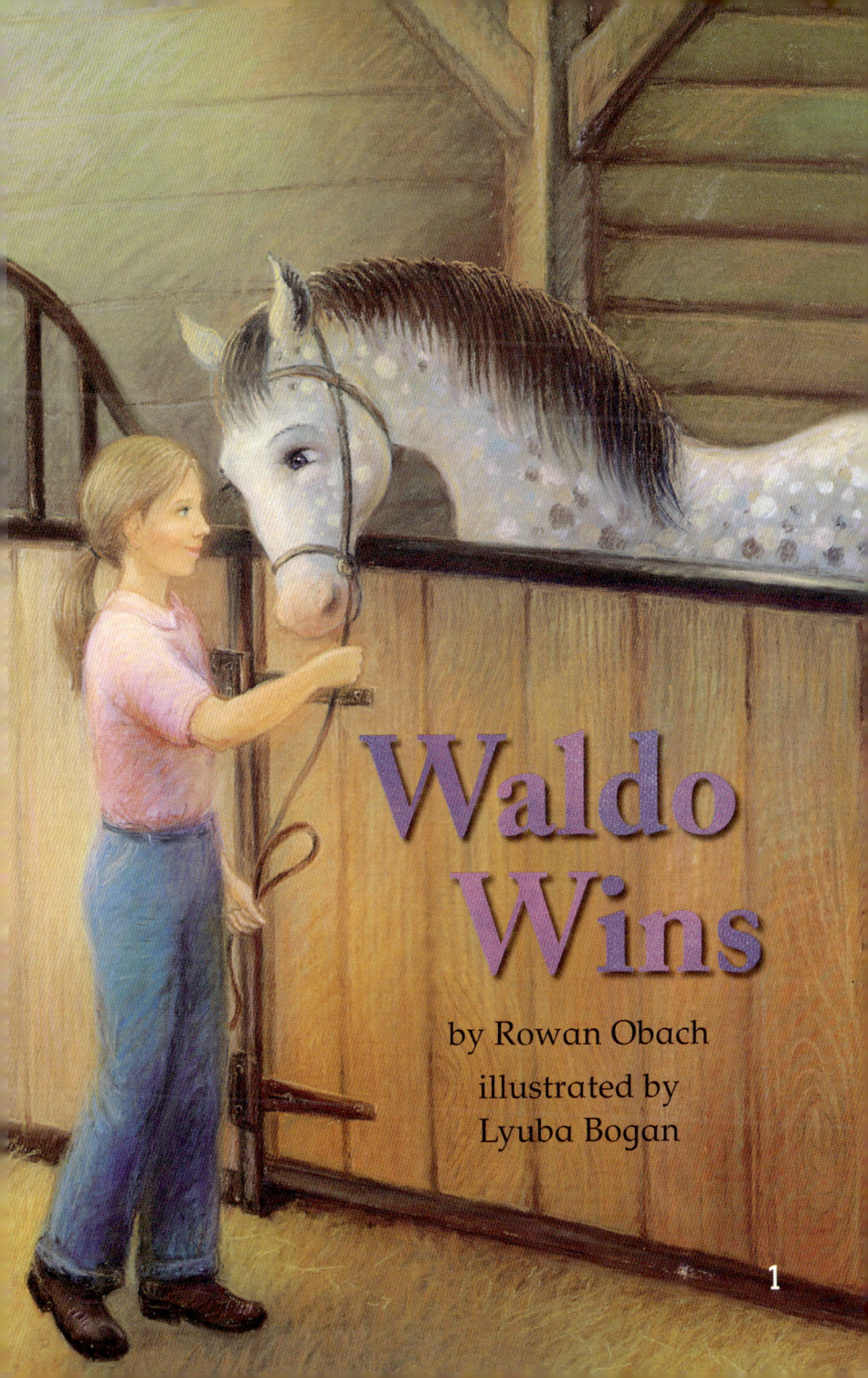

Waldo Wins

by Rowan Obach

illustrated by Lyuba Bogan

Sandy lived on Baldwin Farm. All kinds of horses stayed on the farm. Sandy helped tend the horses. She cleaned the barn stalls. She cleaned and fed the horses. She walked them, holding their halters. She talked to each horse.

Sandy liked all the horses, but she did not have her own horse.

One day, Uncle Dalton came by the farm. He had brought a surprise for Sandy. He thought she might like it. The surprise was a small horse with black and white spots.

Sandy called her horse Waldo. She put him in the best stall. All the other horses got salt blocks, but Waldo always got apples, too.

Sandy thought Waldo was the best horse on the farm. She thought that she and Waldo might win in a riding contest. Uncle Dalton also thought they could win, so Sandy bought a ticket for the contest.

On the day of the contest, big rain squalls hit. The contest was called off for that day.

The next day brought sunny skies. Sandy and Waldo went to the contest ring. They waited in a stall with tall walls. Sandy checked Waldo's halter one last time.

When Sandy's name was called, she and Waldo rode into the ring. They followed the chalk track and jumped all the hurdles.

A boy tossed a beach ball up in the stands, but Waldo kept on walking. The ball did not bother him at all.

Sandy and Waldo halted by the judges' table. Sandy had the best score of all the riders. She and Waldo got first prize.

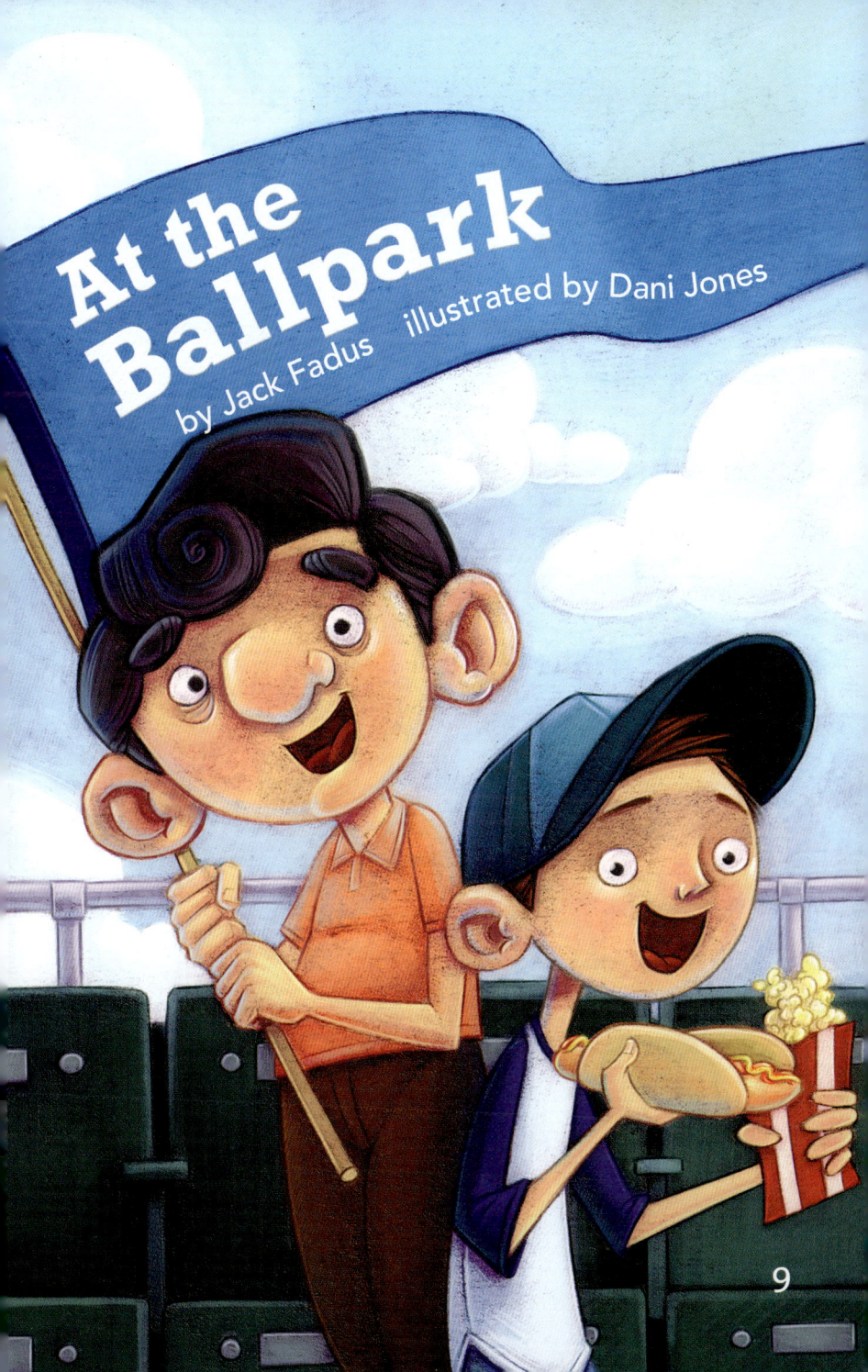

It was the day of the big baseball game. Team flags waved on tall poles over the ballpark walls.

Fans rushed in past the ballpark gates. Some fans brought mitts. Those fans thought they might catch a ball. Some fans brought banners. Those fans thought they might get on TV.

Before the ballgame, players stood at the wall. They talked with fans and wrote their names on balls that fans brought with them.

Fans bought hot dogs and drinks at the food stalls. Fans bought popcorn with salt. Fans bought team shirts and team banners at other stalls.

The team from Elmwood was up at bat first. The pitcher stood up tall on the mound. The batter stood at home plate. The ump stood behind him, ready to call balls and strikes.

"Play ball!" the ump called. The ballgame began.

In the first inning, a batter hit the ball. The ball fell on the white chalk line near first base. "Fair ball!" called the ump. The batter ran to first base.

The coach of the Hillsville team walked out to talk to his pitcher. "You ought to throw the ball lower," he said. "That makes it hard to hit." Then he walked back in the dugout.

The pitcher threw fastballs and curveballs. All of them were low. The Elmwood team could not hit the ball. They could not score.

The Hillsville team hit three home runs over the tall wall in left field. They scored six times to win the game.

All the Hillsville fans cheered. They thought they had the best team in baseball.

Waldo Wins
Word Count: 267

High-Frequency Words

by
have
holding
into
kinds
lived
of
one
other
put
table
their
they
to
too
was

Decodable Words*

a
all
also
always
and
apples
at
Baldwin
ball
barn
beach
best
big
black
blocks
bother
bought
boy
brought
but
called
came
chalk
checked
cleaned

contest
could
Dalton
day
did
each
farm
fed
first
followed
for
got
had
halted
halter
halters
he
helped
her
him
hit
horse
horses
hurdles
in

Boldface words indicate sound-spelling introduced in this story.

(continued)

Decodable Words*

it	skies	**Waldo**
judges	**small**	**Waldo's**
jumped	so	**walked**
kept	spots	**walking**
last	**squalls**	**walls**
like	**stall**	went
liked	**stalls**	when
might	stands	white
name	stayed	win
next	sunny	wins
not	surprise	with
off	**talked**	
on	**tall**	
own	tend	
prize	that	
rain	the	
riders	them	
riding	**thought**	
ring	ticket	
rode	time	
salt	tossed	
Sandy	track	
Sandy's	Uncle	
score	up	
she	waited	

*Boldface words indicate sound-spelling introduced in this story.

At the Ballpark
Word Count: 270

High-Frequency Words

field
from
of
other
said
some
their
they
to
was
were

Decodable Words*

a	cheered
all	coach
and	could
at	**curveballs**
back	day
ball	dogs
ballgame	drinks
ballpark	dugout
balls	Elmwood
banners	fair
base	fans
baseball	**fastballs**
bat	fell
batter	first
before	flags
began	food
behind	game
best	gates
big	get
bought	had
brought	hard
call	he
called	Hillsville
catch	him
chalk	his

*Boldface words indicate sound-spelling introduced in this story.

(continued)

Decodable Words*

hit	players	three
home	poles	threw
hot	popcorn	throw
in	ran	times
inning	ready	TV
it	runs	ump
left	rushed	up
line	**salt**	**walked**
low	score	**wall**
lower	scored	**walls**
makes	shirts	waved
might	six	white
mitts	**stalls**	win
mound	stood	with
names	strikes	wrote
near	**talk**	you
not	**talked**	
on	**tall**	
ought	team	
out	that	
over	the	
past	them	
pitcher	then	
plate	those	
play	**thought**	

*Boldface words indicate sound-spelling introduced in this story.